THE INSIDE STORY OF
EARTH

SUN ☉

MARS

MERCURY ☿

VENUS ♀

EARTH ⊕

00111111111 00000000000 111111111 00000000000001111111100000000000

Sally Ride
Science

EARTH

The Terrestrial Planets

CONTENTS

[1] EARTH: OUR HOME PLANET

Earth and its neighbors in space all share the same Sun. But our home planet is very different from every other place in our solar system.

Just look at Earth. It's blue! Our planet is special because of its deep, blue oceans. No other planet has water flowing on its surface. Water made Earth a living world. So far, it's the only place we know of where life exists—and it's the only place in the solar system where you could live!

Today, a breathable atmosphere surrounds our planet, five oceans cover much of its surface, and seven broad continents cover the rest. And life is everywhere. Earth, our home planet, is an oasis in space.

The Facts

Distance from Sun	149,597,890 kilometers (93 million miles)
Diameter	12,756 kilometers (7,926 miles)
Mass	5.97×10^{24} kilograms
Length of Day (rotation period)	23 hours, 56 minutes
Length of Year (orbit period)	365.3 days
Moons	1

Here's the Lineup

Follow the lineup of our solar system. The sizes of the Sun and the planets are to scale. The Sun is much, much, bigger than anything else in our solar system. The four planets closest to the Sun—Mercury, Venus, Earth, and Mars—are called the "terrestrial planets," because they have solid, rocky surfaces like Earth. They are very different from the next four planets. These "giant planets" are much larger, are made mostly of gas, and don't have solid surfaces to stand on.

Down to Earth

Gravity is the force that keeps you stuck firmly on Earth. The massive Earth tugs on you and keeps you from floating away. Gravity is also the reason that water runs downhill, that apples fall from trees, and that no matter how high you throw a ball, it always comes back down. The effects of Earth's gravity are even felt in space—gravity is what keeps the International Space Station (and the astronauts inside it) in orbit around our planet.

Earth's Birth

A very, very long time ago—about 4.6 billion years ago—a cloud of swirling gas collapsed and formed a shining star and its family of planets. The Sun, Earth, and the other worlds in our solar system formed when material from this cloud collided and began to stick together.

At first, Earth was a giant ball of hot, liquid rock, with no oceans or atmosphere. As Earth began to cool off, volcanoes still erupted across the surface, and it was smashed again and again by rocky meteors and icy comets. Steam and other gases escaped into the air, creating an early atmosphere. Water condensed to form clouds, and torrential rains filled the oceans. It was a nasty place with no trace of life—yet.

This drawing shows how early Earth might have looked about four billion years ago.

Is Earth Made of Earth?

There is a lot more than just dirt beneath your feet! Earth is made up of three major layers: a dense, mostly iron core; a thick, partially molten mantle surrounding the core; and a thin, rocky crust.

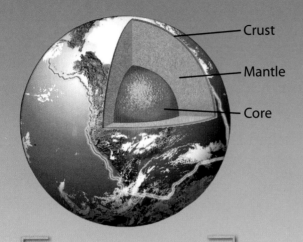

Crust

Mantle

Core

> Earth's crust is a thin skin over our planet, like the skin of an apple.

4 U 2 Do

Soccer Ball Sun

Imagine that the Sun is the size of a soccer ball. Then Earth would be the size of a tiny little pea! Grab a soccer ball and a pea, and you can start to lay out your own mini solar system. Put the soccer ball Sun on the ground. How far away should you put Earth?

Earth is 150 million kilometers from the Sun or about 107 solar diameters. So if the "Sun" is about 23 centimeters (9 inches) across, Earth would be about 24.5 meters (about 80 feet) away! Now, don't let anyone kick the Sun.

The Dirt on Dirt

The dirt, or soil, that covers much of the land forms over thousands of years. It forms when rocks are worn down by rain, ice, sunlight, and wind. Since it's the weather that does it, the process is called weathering. Living things do their part, too. Plants break down rocks by wrenching them apart with their roots. Worms and insects loosen the soil and let in air as they wiggle and dig in the ground. And when plants and animals die and decay, they leave behind minerals and organic molecules that enrich the soil.

Geochemist
University of Arizona

Joaquin Ruiz studies the chemistry of Earth's rocks. He works like a detective. "Being a scientist is one profession where imagination is key," Joaquin tells Sally Ride Science. Joaquin reads the clues contained in each rock. He solves the mystery of when and how a rock formed and of what's happened to it over its lifetime. That can be billions of years!

Joaquin likes to figure out why certain minerals are found in certain parts of the world, such as gold in South Africa and copper in Arizona, where he lives. "What interests me is, when did these deposits form?" Joaquin says.

How Do They Know?

Tick, Tock

Some chemicals in rocks work like clocks. These radioactive elements decay at a steady rate, giving off radiation and turning into other elements. The clock starts ticking when a rock forms. By measuring the very slow decay of some radioactive elements scientists have figured out that Earth formed nearly 4.6 billion years ago. That's a lot of birthday candles!

View from Up, Up

What would you see of Earth from space? Since people began traveling to space in the 1960s, looking down on Earth has been a favorite thing to do. Astronauts on the Apollo 8 mission took photographs as they traveled around the Moon at a distance of 385,000 kilometers (239,000 miles) away from Earth. Astronauts on the Space Shuttle are just 322 kilometers (200 miles) above Earth and can see only part of our planet at any time, but what a view! Looking at Earth from space isn't just about pretty pictures. It gives us a unique perspective and helps us understand Earth better as a whole.

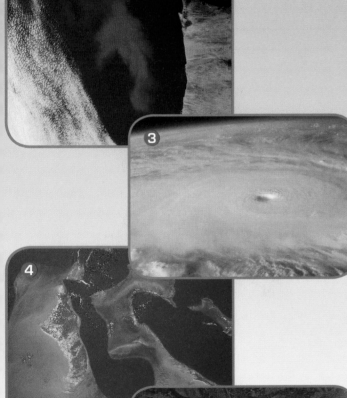

1 From the Moon, our planet sparkles against the blackness of space.

2 Billions of tiny ocean plants, called phytoplankton, add a green color to the ocean.

3 A huge cyclone swirls around its eye—the calm, cloudless center—in the Indian Ocean.

4 The Bahama Islands are surrounded by shallow water (light blue), but it drops off steeply into deep ocean (dark blue).

5 The Rhone River in France empties its cloudy, polluted water into the Mediterranean Sea.

WATER WORLD

Should Planet Earth Be Called "Planet Water"?

One precious substance that has been part of Earth since its very beginning is water. Water is crucial for life. It also plays a major role in shaping just about every natural feature on our planet, from the tallest mountains to the deepest valleys. Water covers 70 percent of Earth, so the surface of our planet is less "earth" than it is "water"! Water makes Earth different from any of the other planets in our solar system. Some people think we should call Earth "the water planet."

This map shows the elevation of land and ocean floor on Earth.

Deep, Deeper, Deepest

The depth of the ocean varies—from shallow beaches to deep seas. The ocean floor has trenches that are deeper than the Grand Canyon. Water in the deepest trench, the Marianas Trench in the South Pacific Ocean, is over 10,000 meters (six miles) deep. That is *really* deep water. If the tallest mountain on Earth, Mount Everest, was placed in that trench, it would be completely underwater.

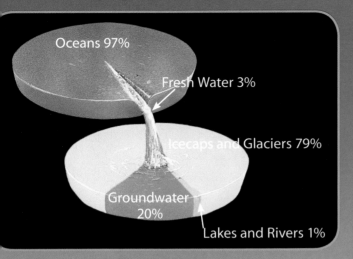

Oceans 97%

Fresh Water 3%

Icecaps and Glaciers 79%

Groundwater 20%

Lakes and Rivers 1%

Almost all the water on our planet is in the saltwater oceans. The rest is fresh water. The diagram at left shows the amount of salt water and fresh water on Earth. It also shows the different forms of fresh water: frozen in icecaps and glaciers, flowing in rivers and lakes, and pooled underground.

Motion of the Ocean

The oceans are not just giant pools of water. The water is constantly on the move. It rises and falls with the tides. Winds kick up waves. And huge currents move rivers of salt water around the planet. The Gulf Stream is an ocean current that flows up the east coast of the United States. It carries warm water from the tropics to the colder North Atlantic Ocean. As it travels north, it loses some of its heat to the air. Without it the tropics would be much hotter, and the poles would be much colder. And guess what—this current carries more water than all the rivers on Earth combined!

How Do They Know?

No Rope Needed

Imagine trying to map the heights of the mountains, canyons, and valleys near you by lowering a rope from an airplane every few miles! That's how sailors used to map the ocean floor. They'd throw a rope over the side of a ship, and when the weight at the end hit bottom, they'd measure how much rope they'd let out.

Today, scientists use a more high-tech form of measurement—sonar (sound waves). They measure the time it takes for sound to travel from a ship to the bottom of the ocean and back again. Sound zips through the ocean at 1,500 meters (almost one mile) a second, so it doesn't take long. But the oceans are immense. So it will be a long time before there's a map of all the mountains and trenches on the ocean floor.

The Gulf Stream is the red curl along the east coast of the United States. This photograph has been colored to show temperature. The warmest water is colored red and orange, and the coldest is colored blue and green.

H₂O Loop

Earth's water is moving all the time. It falls as rain, flows in rivers, evaporates from the surface of oceans and lakes and returns to the air—and is ready to fall to Earth again as rain. That constant loop is called the water cycle. It's powered by the Sun. If you've ever hung wet clothes out to dry, you've seen the heat of the Sun in action. Water can exist as liquid, solid, and vapor. A slippery patch of ice (a solid) can melt to form a puddle (liquid), which evaporates into the air (vapor), then returns to Earth as rain (liquid).

Agassiz Glacier

Hubbard Glacier

Malaspina Glacier

GULF OF ALASKA

Water can spend just days stored as vapor in a cloud, or hundreds of thousands of years locked up as ice in a glacier.

Weather Without Water?

Without water, there would be no weather as we know it. For example, when water falls, or precipitates, from the atmosphere, it comes down as rain, snow, sleet, or hail. The movement of water in the atmosphere, powered by the Sun and pushed by the wind, transports heat around the globe and affects temperatures around the planet.

Experts Tell Us — Dawn Wright

Geographer
Oregon State University

Dawn Wright maps Earth's last frontier: its oceans. Oceans cover 70 percent of Earth, but scientists have explored only 1 percent of the ocean floor in detail. While many geographers stick to land, Dawn loves water. "I grew up in Hawaii and always preferred the ocean," she tells Sally Ride Science.

Dawn studies spots on the ocean floor where molten rock oozes out through cracks in Earth's crust. There, magma can pile up and form soaring, underwater towers that spew hot water. These hydrothermal vents often support rich colonies of sea life. Some people think life first got started around such vents. Dawn has taken three dives in *Alvin*, a submarine that's been used to explore the deep ocean. Can you guess why she's called "Deepsea Dawn"?

[3] EARTH'S BUBBLE OF AIR

Earth is wrapped in a bubble of gases called the atmosphere. The atmosphere stretches high above Earth's surface, and gets thinner and thinner the higher you go. By about 80 kilometers (50 miles) up, there's very little air left. Air is mostly made up of a gas called nitrogen, with a smaller amount of oxygen. It also contains very small amounts of other gases, such as carbon dioxide and water vapor.

There are only traces of water vapor and carbon dioxide in the air, but both are crucial to our climate. They are "greenhouse gases"—they absorb the heat that Earth radiates back toward space and trap it in the atmosphere. Earth's natural greenhouse effect is a good thing. Without it, every place on Earth would be about 16°C (60°F) colder. You'd need a snow shovel in Hawaii!

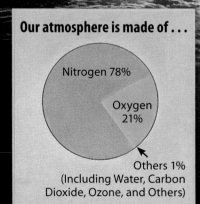

Our atmosphere is made of . . .

Nitrogen 78%

Oxygen 21%

Others 1%
(Including Water, Carbon Dioxide, Ozone, and Others)

Want Oxygen?

Oxygen combines very easily with other elements. So why is there any oxygen in Earth's air? Shouldn't it all have combined with other elements by now? There is oxygen in the air because living things constantly re-supply it. Plants and some microorganisms use the energy in sunlight and carbon dioxide in the air to make their own food. As part of this process, called photosynthesis, oxygen is released into the air. Other planets don't have oxygen in their atmospheres because they don't have life to keep the supply going. Thanks, plants!

Hello, Ozone

Although there is very little ozone in Earth's atmosphere, it is very important to life. Without ozone, too much ultraviolet light would reach the surface of our planet and damage living cells.

Is It Climate or Weather?

It's all a matter of time. Weather is how the atmosphere acts over a short period of time—minutes to months. We talk about today's weather or this winter's weather. Climate is how the atmosphere behaves over long periods of time—years or decades. If summers are hotter now than they were when your parents were children, then that's a change in the climate. If you needed sunscreen yesterday but an umbrella today, that's a change in the weather.

4

THE VIOLENT EARTH

A Jigsaw-Puzzle Planet

The surface of Earth is made up of about a dozen giant plates, each a huge slab of crust. These plates, some as big as continents, float on a molten layer of rock. Heat from inside Earth causes the plates to slide over, under, away from, or past each other. The movement of the plates, called plate tectonics, means that the surface of Earth is constantly changing, although usually too slowly for you to notice.

Even Slower than Molasses

The giant plates move around at speeds of between one and ten centimeters (0.4 to four inches) a year. That's about as fast as your fingernails grow!

The San Andreas Fault is the largest fault in California. It forms a line from the lower right to the top of the picture. No rumbling, please.

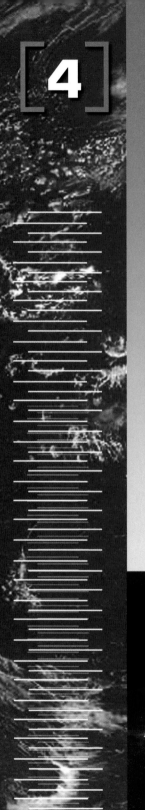

Shake, Rattle, or Roll

Sometimes our planet shakes, rattles, or rolls. Why? Because of plate tectonics. When Earth's gigantic plates collide, spread apart, or slide past one another, that motion can release massive amounts of energy. The result is violent vibrations—earthquakes. Most earthquakes occur at the boundaries between plates. One example is the San Andreas Fault in California, where the Pacific plate is sliding northwest past the plate that holds North America.

How Much Shaking Is Going On?

Lots. There are probably several million earthquakes around the world each year. Most are in remote areas or are too small for us to notice. The magnitude of an earthquake is a measure of its strength—how much energy it releases. Each increase of one magnitude means an earthquake is ten times stronger. So an earthquake of magnitude 5 is ten times stronger than one of magnitude 4. Luckily, big quakes are as rare as small quakes are common. In a typical year, Earth experiences

- one quake larger than magnitude 8.0.
- over 1,000,000 quakes between magnitude 2.0 and 2.9.

Mini and Mega

The smallest quake you would notice would be about magnitude 3.5. The most powerful earthquake ever recorded was a monster quake—magnitude 9.5!—that hit Chile in 1960.

That's a Lot of Hot!

When plates spread apart or crash together, molten magma or lava, hot ash, and gas can escape to the surface. That's a volcano! There are about 500 active volcanoes around the world, not counting those found under the ocean. More than half of the world's volcanoes are located around the edges of the Pacific Ocean, forming what's called the "Ring of Fire."

Experts Tell Us   Tina Neal

Volcanologist
United States Geological Survey

Tina Neal keeps an eye on the 43 active volcanoes in Alaska, sometimes traveling around the rugged state by airplane or helicopter. Tina and other scientists at the Alaska Volcano Observatory alert others to the dangers of erupting volcanoes. Even small eruptions can be dangerous, since ash in the air can gum up the engines of jet airplanes flying overhead. In college, Tina set her heart on studying volcanoes on other planets. Later, in graduate school, she worked on Mount St. Helens in Washington State during several small eruptions of the volcano. "That was all I needed to study active volcanoes here on Earth," she tells Sally Ride Science.

Tina studies a collapsed volcano in Alaska.

Deep and Tall

Mountains also form on the bottom of the ocean. As two plates pull apart, molten rock rises from below to create new crust that fills the gap. That can lead to the creation of new mountains. The Mid-Atlantic Ridge is a mostly underwater mountain range that runs under the Atlantic Ocean for about 16,000 kilometers (10,000 miles). Some of the mountains are high enough to poke out of the water and form islands, such as the Azores off the coast of Portugal (photographs above).

Grow Your Own Mountains

How do mountains get so high? Let your hands show you. Just place your hands flat on a table, with your fingers pointing toward each other. Pretend your hands are separate tectonic plates. Now gently slide them together and watch how your fingers bend upward when they collide. Congratulations, you've built a mountain range just like the Himalayas! Now try it again, but this time let the fingers of one hand slide under the fingers of the other hand. The fingers on top should rise up to form a mountain range more like the Andes.

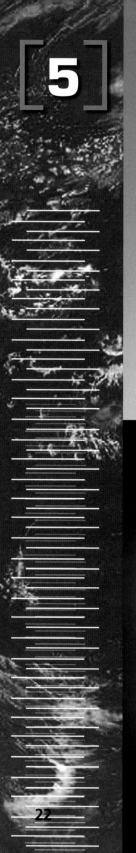

5

ENERGIZED EARTH

Our Bright Best Friend

We couldn't exist without the Sun. The Sun provides Earth with most of the energy that makes it go. The Sun's heat and light make plants grow and winds blow. The Sun isn't unique, though. It's one of hundreds of billions of stars in our galaxy. Even though it's 150 million kilometers (93 million miles) away, it's by far the closest star to Earth—and our biggest and brightest neighbor.

Sixty Minutes, Six Billion

Earth receives more energy from the Sun in one hour than all six billion of us use during an entire year.

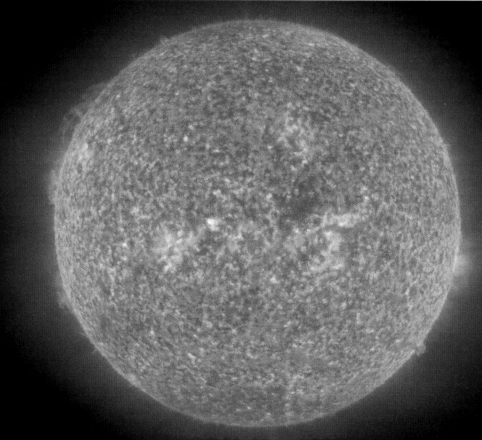

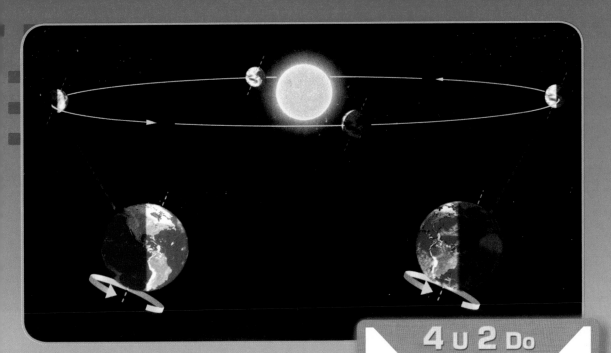

Why Can't It Be Summer All Year 'Round?

Like a slightly crooked lampshade, Earth isn't quite straight. It's slightly tilted. It's because of that tilt that we have four different seasons: winter, spring, summer, and fall. Here's why: in one part of the year, the northern half of the planet is tipped toward the Sun (above, lower right). This means more sunshine and higher temperatures—summer! During this same time, the southern hemisphere (everything south of the equator) is tipped away from the Sun—time for winter coats. Six months later, the northern hemisphere is tipped away from the Sun (above, lower left), so it's winter there and summer in the south.

If It's Noon on Your Nose . . .

Earth takes 24 hours, or one day, to rotate once on its axis, that imaginary line that runs between the north and south poles. When it's daytime for the half of the planet that faces the Sun, it's nighttime for the half that faces away from the Sun. You can simulate this by going into a dark room that's lit by only one lamp. Pretend that you're Earth and the lamp is the Sun. Face the lamp and slowly turn in place counterclockwise, just like Earth. When your nose points to the lamp, it's "noon" on your nose, "dawn" at your right ear, and "midnight" on the back of your head! Turn one quarter rotation more, and it's now "noon" on your right ear.

What Makes the World Go Around?

Our planet gets a huge amount of light and heat from the Sun—but it's hard to harness that energy for our everyday needs. Some homes and cars run on solar power, but most of our energy for electricity and heat comes from burning fossil fuels—coal, oil, and gas. Fossil fuels are formed over millions of years from the remains of ancient plants and animals (even dinosaurs). When oil and coal are taken from the ground, they can be burned to light and heat our homes and make our cars, planes, and trains go. Thanks, dinos!

Heating Up

Temperatures around the world have risen especially quickly in the last 100 years. Scientists believe humans are mostly responsible. Whenever we burn wood or fossil fuels, carbon dioxide, a greenhouse gas, is released into the atmosphere. There it acts like a blanket that wraps Earth and keeps some heat from escaping into space. With more and more people on the planet, more and more carbon dioxide is being added to the atmosphere every day.

Fill 'er Up . . . and Up and Up

The average person in the United States uses about 1,800 liters (475 gallons) of gasoline, a fossil fuel, every year!

Space Shuttle astronauts took this photograph of Earth's atmosphere at sunrise. Huge thunderclouds rise high into the orange and yellow sky.

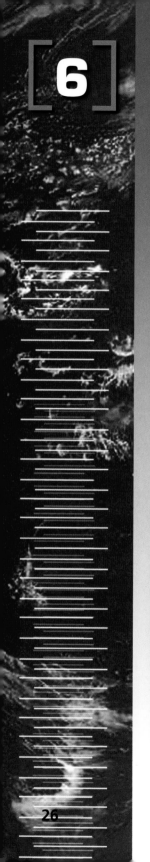

[6] LIFE!

The Recipe for Life

We know life on Earth began when our planet was only about one billion years old. Then, as now, Earth had the three ingredients—energy, organic molecules, and water—that life requires. The building blocks of life formed on early Earth when key molecules came together in the right combinations and under the right conditions. The first forms of life were simple, single-celled, microscopic organisms. These organisms slowly evolved over billions of years to form more and more complex creatures—all the way from bacteria to blue whales. We don't yet know if life exists anywhere else in the Universe—so for now, we're special.

The Biosphere Gets Bigger

The biosphere is the portion of Earth that is home to life. It includes land, water, and air. Life is found everywhere on Earth where there is even a trace of water. We find life in amazing places, including deep beneath the surface of the planet and in places both boiling hot (deepsea hydrothermal vents) and freezing cold (Antarctica).

This deepsea hydrothermal vent on the bottom of the Atlantic Ocean is home to heat-loving bacteria and other living creatures.

Meet the Beetles

We don't know how many different species of living things there are. Estimates range from just two million to around 80 million. Some think that beetles may make up a quarter of all species!

4 U 2 Do

Wet and Weird

From the seashore to the seafloor, the oceans are loaded with life—and new species are being discovered all the time. Can you match the descriptions with the choices below?

1. What huge, warm-blooded animals sing to each other to stay in touch?

2. This deepsea animal has one big eye that looks up for food and one small eye that looks down for predators.

3. Towering forests found off the coast of California. What are the plants seen here that can grow 38 meters (125 feet) long?

4. Usually these creatures feed by filtering small bits of food from the water. Recently discovered, this one engulfs other organisms with their "mouths."

5. Since these red fish live too deep for light to reach them, they appear gray and blend with the shadows, hiding from prey.

a) Giant kelp
b) Rosy rockfish
c) Blue whales
d) Wonky-eyed jewel squid
e) Carnivorous sponges

Check out your answers on page 32.

Life Shapes Earth

Life has adapted to Earth, but did you know that life has changed Earth, too? Here are some examples.

1. Early bacteria, similar to today's cyanobacteria, were the first forms of life to perform photosynthesis. Over the ages, they helped supply the oxygen in our air. This allowed for the evolution of animals that breathe oxygen, like you!

2. In the tropics, living corals form reefs that turn into small islands.

3. Giant limestone mountains are formed from the remains of tiny sea creatures that sank to the bottom of the ocean. Fossils of these sea creatures are found all over the globe, even on top of Mount Everest!

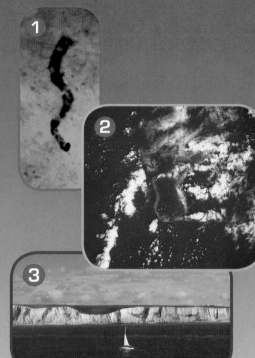

Mega-Time

To understand Earth's history, you have to think in mega-units of time—much, much longer than those you'd use to talk about your own life. Instead of days, months, and years, you have to think in hundreds of millions and even billions of years.

How Do They Know?

Mega-Time

To understand Earth's history, you have to think in mega-units of time—much, much longer than those you'd use to talk about your own life. Instead of days, months, and years, you have to think in hundreds of millions and even billions of years.

This fossil moth was found in China. Its body is about 2.5 centimeters (one inch) long and its wings are about five centimeters (two inches) across. It lived about 125 million years ago.

What Can I Do?

You are one of over six billion humans living on our planet. Each of us depends on Earth. We depend on it for the air we breathe, the water we drink, the food we eat, and the land we live on. And we share it with all the other amazing living things that call Earth home.

We humans are especially clever at figuring out ways to shape the environment to meet our needs. We cut down trees, mine metals, pump water, and drill for fossil fuels like no other creature on Earth.

Our planet has supported life for a very long time. How do we keep it that way? We care about our planet. And we keep learning about its air, water, land, and life, and how they work together to keep Earth a livable world.

THE HISTORY OF
EARTH

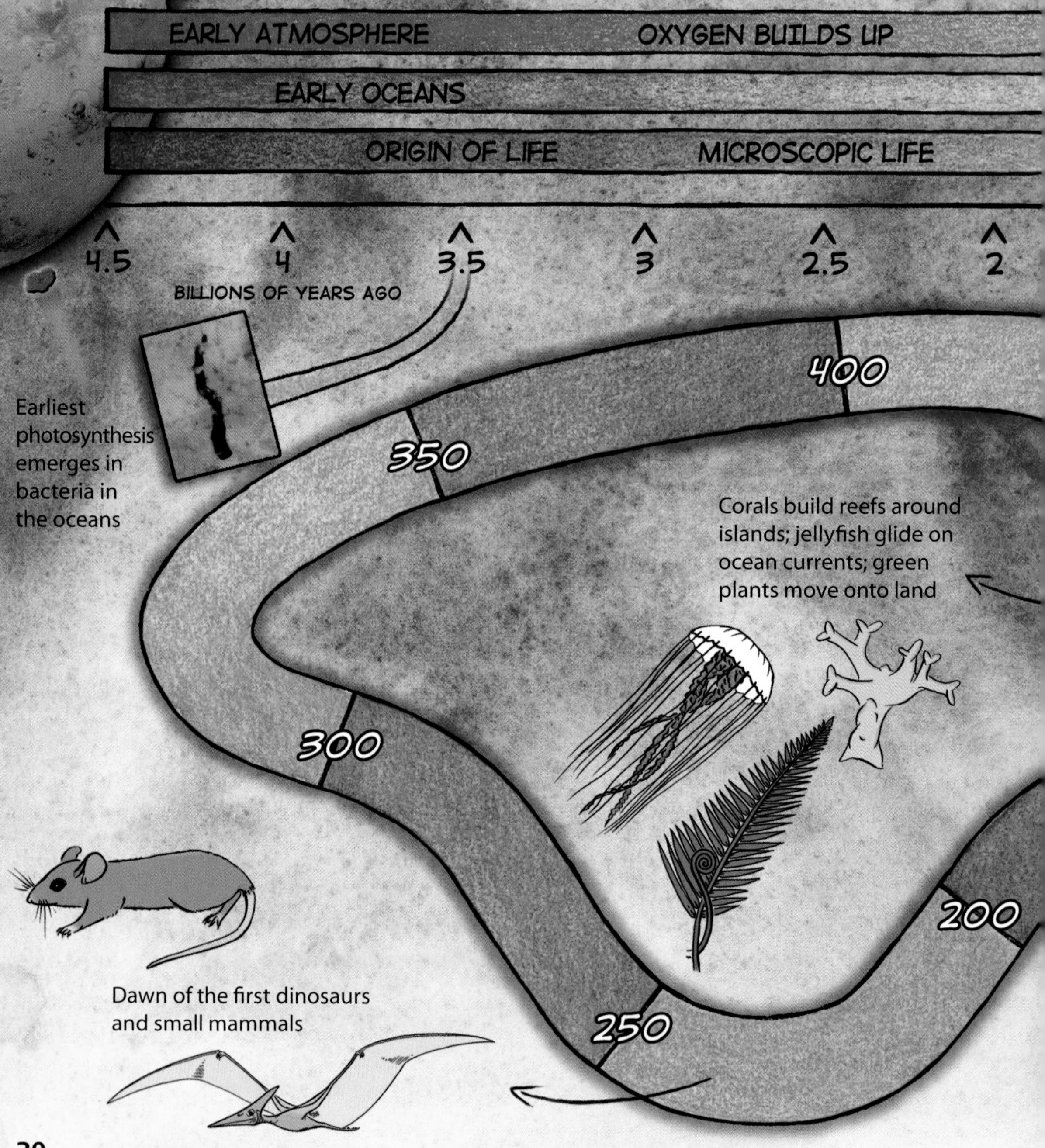

EARLY ATMOSPHERE	OXYGEN BUILDS UP
EARLY OCEANS	
ORIGIN OF LIFE	MICROSCOPIC LIFE

^   ^   ^   ^   ^   ^
4.5   4   3.5   3   2.5   2

BILLIONS OF YEARS AGO

Earliest photosynthesis emerges in bacteria in the oceans

400

350

Corals build reefs around islands; jellyfish glide on ocean currents; green plants move onto land

300

200

250

Dawn of the first dinosaurs and small mammals

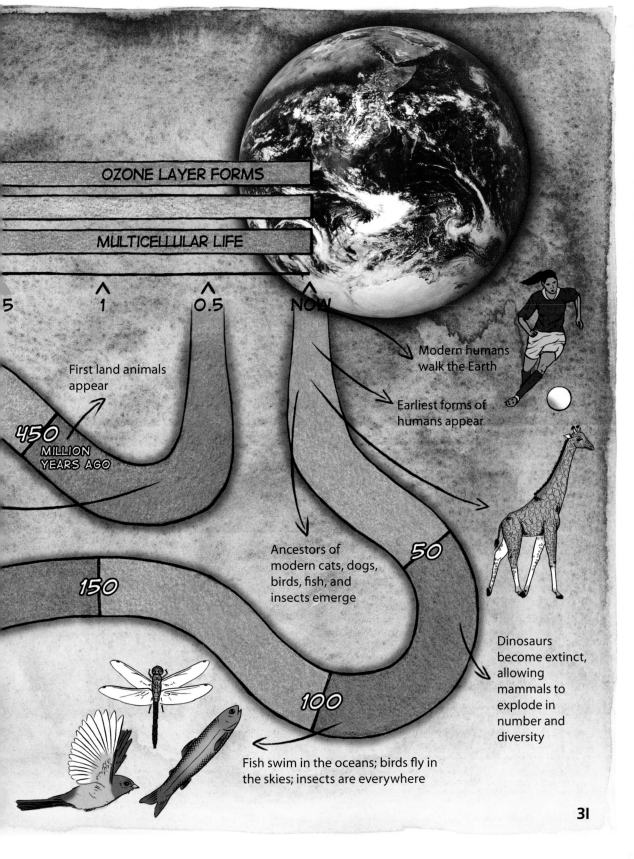

OZONE LAYER FORMS

MULTICELLULAR LIFE

5   1   0.5   NOW

Modern humans walk the Earth

Earliest forms of humans appear

First land animals appear

450 MILLION YEARS AGO

Ancestors of modern cats, dogs, birds, fish, and insects emerge

50

150

100

Dinosaurs become extinct, allowing mammals to explode in number and diversity

Fish swim in the oceans; birds fly in the skies; insects are everywhere

31

atmosphere (n.) A layer of gas surrounding a planet or moon, held in place by the force of gravity. (pp. 4, 8, 15, 16, 17, 25, 30)

bacteria (n; singular bacterium.) Microscopic organisms with a single cell and no organized cell structures. (pp. 26, 28, 30)

crust (n.) The relatively thin, solid outer layer of a terrestrial planet or a moon. (pp. 9, 15, 18, 21)

current (n.) The movement of a large body of water or air. (p. 13)

element (n.) Any substance that exists in its purest chemical form. (pp. 10, 17)

greenhouse effect (n.) The warming that occurs when certain gases (greenhouse gases) are present in a planet's atmosphere. Visible light from the Sun penetrates the atmosphere of a planet and heats the ground; the warmed ground then radiates infrared radiation back toward space. If greenhouse gases are present, they absorb some of that infrared, trapping it and making the planet warmer than it otherwise would be. (p. 16)

magma (n.) Molten rock beneath a planet's crust. (pp. 15, 20)

microscopic organism (n; also known as microbe.) A form of life, usually single-celled, that is too small to be seen without a microscope. (p. 26)

orbit (n.) The path of one body around another, as a result of the force of gravity between them. Examples are a planet's path around the Sun or a moon's path around a planet. (p. 7)

photosynthesis (n.) Process by which plants use energy from sunlight to convert carbon dioxide and water into food (in the form of sugar). Oxygen is released in the process. (pp. 17, 26, 30)

plate tectonics (n.) The Earth's crust is broken into large sections called plates. Plate tectonics describes their constant motion relative to each other, and explains the geologic activity and recycling of the crust that occurs as a result. (pp. 18, 19, 21)

INDEX

Answers

4 U 2 Do, page 27

1. c   4. e
2. d   5. b
3. a